FINDING MY WAY IN CHRIST

Who Am I?

How Am I?

Where Am I?

What Am I doing?

Why Am I going
through this?

Copyrighted Material

Copyright © 2017
Date of publication January 2017
Authored by Dr. Derrick Lamont Randolph Sr.
Published by Journey of Faith Ministries
Baltimore, Maryland
United States of America

The character illustrations are works-for-hire.

All concepts, ideas, copy, sketches, art work, electronic files and other materials related to the Journey of Faith are the property of Journey of Faith Ministries.

Journey of Faith Ministries
contact@journeyoffaithministries.org
www.journeyoffaithministries.org

All rights reserved.
This book may not be reproduced in whole or in part by any process without written permission from the copyright holder.

ISBN-13: 978-1-944166-28-1

ISBN-10: 1-944166-28-9

- Who am I? ...15
- How Am I? ...26
- Where am I going? ...52
  - Salvation ...66
  - Church Leadership ...67
  - Leaders ...68
  - Love ...70
  - Marriage ...71
  - PARENTING ...73
  - Friends ...75
  - Opportunities ...76
  - Volunteering ...77
  - Service ...78
  - Skills ...80
  - Job hunting ...82
  - Needs ...83
- What am I doing with my time? ...84
- Why am I going through this? ...93
- When am I going to find my way ...99

Forward

Are we Godless?

The prevalent perception of the African American community is that we are living in a state of inferiority, living God-less and spirit-less, following the cultural traditions that include idol worship, things lauded as gods that are born of our own creativity, but not the true and living God.

Identity-less

It seems we have have lost our identities as we've traveled the slave ships to the Americas, displayed our nakedness on slave blocks; and travailed in the fields of plantation owners. We appeared to be a lost people, displaced, separated and alienated. We have not been exposed to the aristocratic culture of our masters, and it appears that we have lost our identity.

Blind and forgetful

Through recent centuries, we've progressed, but also mis-stepped. Some have amassed fortunes. Yet, while engaging in the busyness of accumulating and emulating, we've forgotten where we've come from and need to get to. We've obtained nobility, but lost our humanity. We have been blinded by the "American Dream" and vision of a fulfilled life. Some live it at the expense of failed relationships, developing dysfunctional, but wealthy families.

Others have existed and held to the family structure. They've learned to survive but live in a substandard quality of life. In the midst of this transition, our generation has splintered into pieces. Some poor and thus sick. Some wealthy, yet sick.

Lacking Social Consciousness

Collectively we are losing our social consciousness. We are in danger of isolating ourselves so every man goes for himself, leaving the concept of community behind. If we lose our sense of community, which is strengthened in our love for each other, self and collective respect, we will cease to be a people. We must preserve our identity, reestablish our community of leadership, of authority, our boundaries and rules within the community.

When we reclaim our community, we will bring into subjection, the pursuit of life, liberty and of happiness. We will reign in the "American Dream," and snuff out the senseless murders, crime, drugs, gang involvement, fraud, embezzlement, the lot. We will restore the purity, the beauty of our people, our community, our habitation and the blossoming flowers that have long been unscathed by the winds and rains of life.

Disconnected

Just imagine, one day our community will no longer forsake the assembling of ourselves on Sunday. We will cherish the opportunity to celebrate the goodness of "the one" God who created you. One day, our non-church goers will remember that God is more than a 'higher power'. They will remember through naturally recognition that God is more than 'the man upstairs". They too will join us to honor God until they become childlike worshippers. I sense that God has a solution for this!

SOLUTION

God has a solution for us, hardcoded in the Word of God. The God breathed scripture is the most valuable resource we could ever possess. It has a wealth of truth to lead and guide us. It has God's prescription that can alleviate any and every problem if we would just put our trust in him. God lays out the path to all truth, to Jesus Christ, and a life in His kingdom, which is amazing and beautiful in its entirety.

To walk in His kingdom, we have to embrace the life in Jesus Christ that God has prepared for us. For, it is in God that we live and breathe and have our very being. The word of God says life is not about that, but peace, love, and joy in the Holy Ghost.

Know and understand that we can be the people that God destined for us to be.

He called us to be "a chosen generation, a royal priesthood, a holy nation, a peculiar people; that Ye should shew forth the praises of him who called you out of darkness into his marvelous light." 1 Peter 2:9.

This is available to this generation.

We will look at who we are as individuals.

Introduction

One thing I realized is how far I've come. When I started out, I did not know how to do much but at the very least, I was very committed to the Lord Jesus Christ. I walked and talked with God. If anyone did not have a similar demonstration of the devotion to God that was similar to mine I felt they were not trying. It took time but I learned that in addition to developing devotion to God I had to develop internal transformation and learn how to implement my love and devotion to God in very different areas of my life.

WHO AM I?

Finding My Identity in Christ

The problem is…

We're on a failed quest for self-identity

Let's look at the problem of our identity. We are broken, lost, struggling, and hurting in a world that hates us. Nothing or no one helps us know who we are. Nothing feeds us the truth of who we are. People long for love but receive abuse. Those in power profit and proliferate the lesser. The world and the powers of this world intentionally show that they don't care about us. It leaves us hurt, lost, marginalized, feeling defeated in this world. We don't know who we are, why we're here, or what we are going to do. We find ourselves in weak moments wondering who we are. Who am I? What am I here for?

The solution is Jesus will reveal your identity

Here is the truth. You are the people of the bible who received the revelation of God. You are the first man and woman, created by God to know God personally. You are Abraham's children who will walk with God by faith. You are the Old Testament Hebrew children who were set free from bondage. You are the Israelites being led to the Promised Land. You are the New Testament Jew and Gentile believers who receive the preaching, teaching and healing ministry of Jesus. You are the New Testament Gentile believers who are established in local churches, who develop communities of faith. You are the beloved community who provide civil rights and live in a bond of unity together. You will become a believer, a witness, a servant, a son, a joint Heir in Jesus Christ, and an ambassador for Christ.

Evolution of Spiritual Transformation

We are Believers

We are Witnesses

We are Servants

We are Friends

We are Ambassadors for Christ

We are Heirs in Jesus Christ

We are Believers

Those who accepted his message were baptized, and about three thousand were added to their number that day. [42] They devoted themselves to the apostles' teaching and to fellowship, to the breaking of bread and to prayer. [43] Everyone was filled with awe at the many wonders and signs performed by the apostles. [44] All the believers were together and had everything in common. [45] They sold property and possessions to give to anyone who had need. [46] Every day they continued to meet together in the temple courts. They broke bread in their homes and ate together with glad and sincere hearts, [47] praising God and enjoying the favor of all the people. And the Lord added to their number daily those who were being saved. (Acts 2:41-47)

We are Witnesses

There was a man sent from God whose name was John. [7] He came as a witness to testify concerning that light, so that through him all might believe. [8] He himself was not the light; he came only as a witness to the light. (John 1:6-8)

But you will receive power when the Holy Spirit comes on you; and you will be my witnesses in Jerusalem, and in all Judea and Samaria, and to the ends of the earth." (Acts 1:8)

We are Servants

"Here is my servant whom I have chosen, the one I love, in whom I delight; I will put my Spirit on him, and he will proclaim justice to the nations. (Matthew 12:18)

We are Friends

Greater love hath no man than this that a man lay down his life for his friends. [14] Ye are my friends, if ye do whatsoever I command you. [15] Henceforth I call you not servants; for the servant knoweth not what his lord doeth: but I have called you friends; for all things that I have heard of my Father I have made known unto you.

John 15:13-15 (KJV)

We are Ambassadors for Christ

To wit, that God was in Christ, reconciling the world unto himself, not imputing their trespasses unto them; and hath committed unto us the word of reconciliation. [20] Now then we are ambassadors for Christ, as though God did beseech you by us: we pray you in Christ's stead, be ye reconciled to God. 2 Corinthians [21] For he hath made him to be sin for us, who knew no sin; that we might be made the righteousness of God in him. 5:19-21 (KJV)

We are Heirs in Jesus Christ

[16] The Spirit itself beareth witness with our spirit, that we are the children of God: [17] And if children, then heirs; heirs of God, and joint-heirs with Christ; if so be that we suffer with him, that we may be also glorified together. [18] For I reckon that the sufferings of this present time are not worthy to be compared with the glory which shall be revealed in us. Romans 8:16-18 (KJV)

How Am I?

(Finding Balance in Christ)

The problem is...

We live on the extremes and need to find the spiritual center of gravity

Learning to Reflect Inward

The funny thing about life is that God will give you balance when you need it. When I reflect on my own life, I've seen how God has balanced me out. For example, in my twenties I was a hip hop (rap) artist. When I rapped, I was very intellectual (Cerebral). I found myself struggling with providing with something tangible that they could connect to and relate to. I rapped with a little bit of bravado, and a little bit of wordplay, shifting and moving my flow to the beat. In time I was introduced to narrating my story and sharing my private struggles. I learned to reflect internally before I'd tell my story. That way you'd get the truth, good, bad or ugly as I exposed myself, my thoughts, feelings, and struggles. In hindsight I can see that God put led me to the people, places and situations that would enlighten me and pull this out of me.

Now as I journey in Christ, I see it occurring almost daily. God balancing my life. Marrying the sensual, feeling part of me and the cerebral part of me. It is easy to dream up a concept, share a thought or vent your opinions. It is an even greater thing to reach down within and tell your story so it blesses someone else. Trust me, God will balance you out.

The Need for Balance

I've transformed from sensual (a person of feelings) to intellectual (more astute), to a place of greater balance between the two. I still love God and people. I've learned to balance emotions with wisdom, to actually live and enjoy life. Yet, I can do so while making informed decisions and controlled actions. The more I learn, grow and talk to others about this balancing act, the more I discover that life is imbalanced for many of us. We lash out in defense and self-preservation when we are given something to ponder on. We contemplate silently in despair when we are expected to engage in thoughtful discussion. We lambast out of frustration when we should listen and learn from criticism. Altogether, we present ourselves as unhealthy.

People feel an ill persona that needs healing. Our Christian witness is at times warped because people see in us a person that needs to be whole. We may grow leaps and bounds in the faith; we may be spiritually in tune to the presence of God and possess the anointing to do great things for Jesus, but when bear the marks of imbalance, our witness only dimly shines the light of Christ to others. There is good news though.

Spirit vs. Work

There is a remedy. Jesus will help you achieve a healthy balance in life. Here's how; we have persons that serve often, all of the time. Others are more diligent workers, but they aren't very spiritual; they just do a lot. Then there are those who are very spiritual, committed and faithful. They are very discerning, able to inspire others to become more attuned to God's spirit but they are otherwise less industrious of good works. Those are two spiritual ends, practical work and spiritual experience. Neither is greater than the other. They are simply different.

Cerebral vs. Sensual

There is another set of extremes. There is the very sensual, with the tendency to interpret life through their feelings. They are convinced that they're on the spiritual side because they feel good. They are in the spirit, on a high, unable to come down and balance out. In all of their sensuality, they lean on the emotional side but they don't develop the cerebral capacity to balance themselves out emotionally. They don't have a sober reality of their Christian walk, and aren't able to diagnose themselves when they err spiritually. The intellectual isn't capable of self-awakening.

They are apt to discern when they are wrong, but aren't able to refocus their energy, passion and drive to head in the right direction. They are dumbed to the flow of spirit and sense of the spirit's direction. This Christian knows right from wrong, when they are right vs. wrong but are unable to fly their kite with the wind. They too need to balance their thinking with some feeling.

The Need for Power

Some of us are blessed with a sober reality, a strong moral compass that allows us to do many things right. We are rarely aware when we mess up. We know how to talk to people and treat people well. We are good with people. We won't do too much to mess up our witness, but we never get power. The spirit of God never completely overwhelms us with power. We're never compelled to receive, experience or be led by the power of God. The power of God is rarely visibly demonstrated in our lives. As a result, people rarely witness, believe and accept the invitation to salvation by the power of God that is alive in this type of Christian. My friends, what lies before us is a difficult balancing act. We've got to find ourselves in the middle somewhere. With every extreme there is a middle ground waiting for us. Find that middle ground. Welcome the refreshing balance of life in Christ. Enjoy the power of God in your ordinary life and watch it transform into extraordinary!

As you experience this, you will have to share yourself, your experience and the power of God with others. Just as you've had to find balance in your own life, you've got to know where people are in order to minister to them. There's a scale of failure, of falling, of weakness. People fall somewhere on the scale. By finding your balance, you will be healthy enough to help others find their balance. Life, it's got to be balanced. I call it a journey of faith, but it's not a journey of faith, it's a scale of faith that is comprised of various small balance scales. There are a lot of small moving parts that make up our spiritual lives that require balance. The complex human, spirit, soul person that you are has to be engaged and growing in various different directions at a time. The good news is that you are not in control of it all. You simple have to be cognizant of it, surrendered to God who will guide you through it all, and focused on loving, obediently doing what is right and required in order to become successful in finding balance. The Lord Jesus will do the rest.

Stay Encouraged

Once you get the spiritual piece down, you may find that you want to stay spiritually high. You may walk in the spirit in a major way, but you will be short somewhere else. The whole part of who you are is made of different parts of you that all need to grow. As you nurture and cultivate different parts of your life, there are certain parts that you can't grow yourself. God will have to balance you out and grow you up, using different life events to shift you in different directions.

You will experience the growth of different personality and character traits. You will watch various gifts and abilities that develop in you, but if you are too far on one side it will be painful. You will still feel an unease, an emptiness. Though you may be able do a variety of spiritual, civil and familial things, if you don't grow the whole person that is in you then it will all be for naught. As a believer, witness, servant, friend, ambassador and heir in Christ, you may cause others to stumble if you don't get balanced. Again, Christian discipleship is more than a journey of faith. It is a balance of faith. You are on a spiritual balance scale and the Lord is looking to balance you out.

The Goal is to balance who you are with what you do!

Find balance within all of your extremities

The person who lives and relates primarily cerebrally should begin to balance themselves with their human sensibilities and vice versa. Likewise, we should balance our propensity to be internally and externally expressive in our faith.

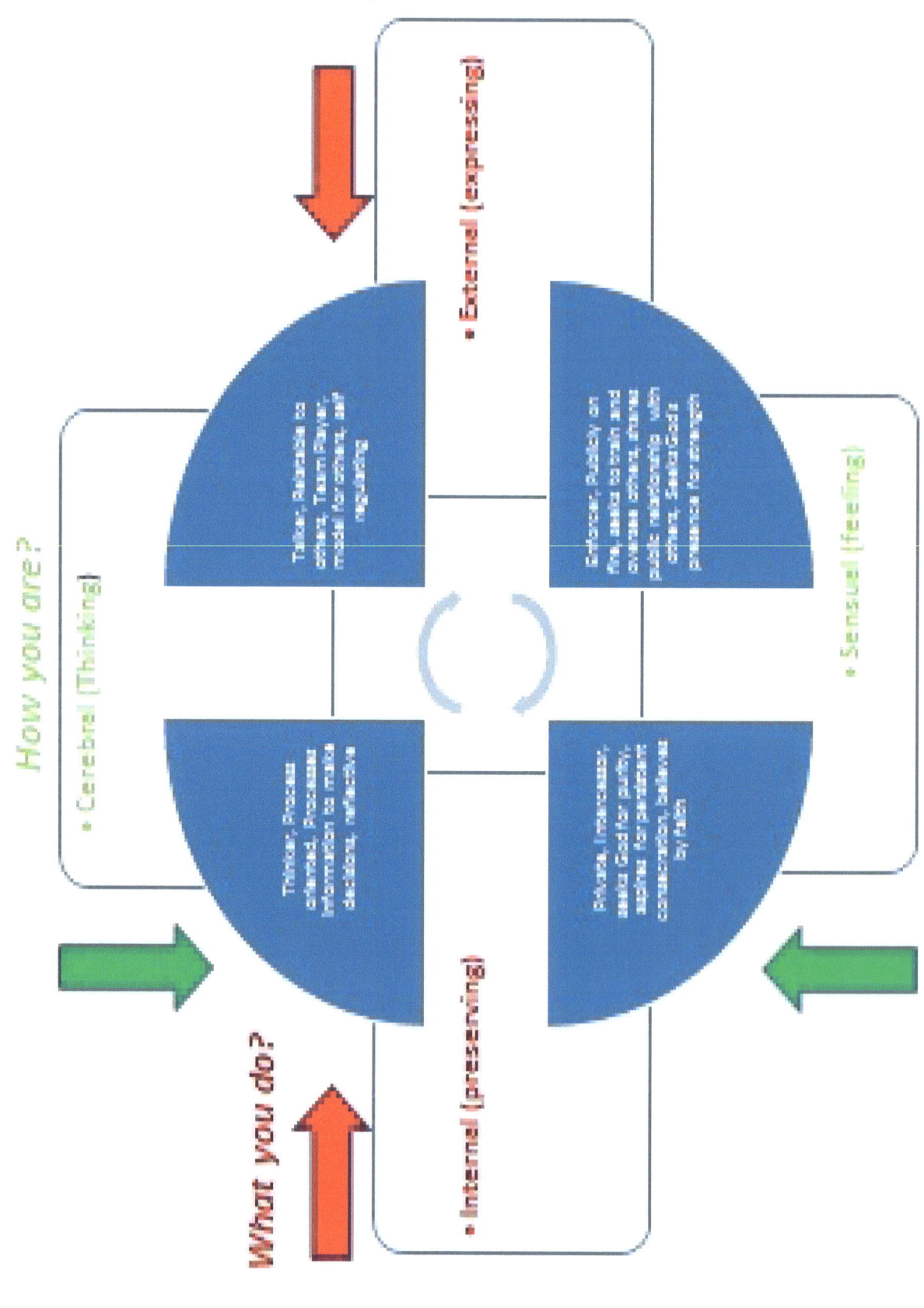

The Goal is to balance how you are in order to achieve maximum power to live!

You should learn to balance how you are. The person who is more cerebral should balance themselves and become sensual and vice versa. That is, the person who lives primarily in a biblical, sober, moral, cerebral, should balance out. That means welcoming the opportunity to become more spiritual, emotional. That may render you less cerebral, productive and practical, thus giving the appearance of being immoral, sensual, idle and ineffectual aspects of Christian living.

Ultimately, the balance of spiritual sensibility and mental capacity will allow you to possess power, operate in accountability, morality, overcoming of sin, righteousness, and pragmatisms.

Balance How You Are

Biblical	Spiritual
Sober	Emotional
Moral	Immoral
Cerebral	Sensual
Productive	Idle
Practical	Ineffectual

- Have Power
- Be Accountable
- Develop Morals
- Overcome Sin
- Be Righteous
- Be Pragmatic

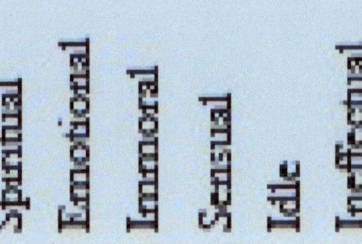
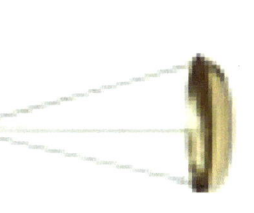

Now, the person who primarily demonstrates faith in Jesus Christ internally should begin to balance themselves with externally expressed demonstrations of faith and vice versa. Likewise, we should balance our expressed demonstrations of faith with internal activities.

Balance What You Do

Internally

- Talk to God (talkative)
- Relatable, relative
- Team player
- Model, self-regulate
- Private relationship enjoyed alone
- Intercessor
- Spiritual Health
- Seek God's presence for comfort
- Pleasure seeker
- Vents
- Trusts God (instincts)
- Seek human leadership for guidance

Externally

- Hear God (listener)
- On fire
- Enforcer
- Train, oversee others
- Public relationship shared with others
- Activism
- Social Justice
- Seek God's presence for strength
- Persistent consecration
- Biblical truths and lessons
- Pursue God for sings and confirmation
- Seek divine revelation

Today's church must be challenged to help believers balance each area of one's health in order to be flexible enough to work with other areas. To achieve balance there are various aspects of your health that requires balance.

Spiritual disciplinary health

Prayerful vs. doubting

Fasting vs. gluttonous

Praise vs. withdrawn

Worshipful vs. denying

Serving vs. selfish

Fellowship vs. standoffish

Emotional health

Self-controlled vs. anxious, hasty

Intellectual health

Astute vs. disoriented

Physical health

Energetic vs. lethargic

Calm vs. frenzied

Balanced Personality

Introvert vs. extrovert

Quiet vs. loud

Balanced Ministry

Inspiration vs Authority

Conclusion

Find balance in your calling to provide inspiration and to exercise authority. Are you called to provide inspiration? Preachers of the gospel provide inspiration. They are the pulpit prognosticators that proclaim the truths of the gospel. They are also the classroom teachers. Are you called to exercise authority over the church? There is the government of the church. God's chosen must manage the affairs of the church. They lead ministries, projects and people. Which are you called to do?

Where am I going?

(Changing and Growing in Christ)

The Problem is...

We don't know where life will lead us

The Solution is...

Jesus has a destination for you; to get there you are required to Change & Grow

God has an eternal destination for us in the kingdom of heaven. God has an existing destination for us right now in the kingdom of God. You need to change and grow to get to the destination that God has for you. You must go through transformation to get to your destination.

Throughout the bible, God used Faith, Law, Love and Power to introduce believers to new ways of living for God. To introduce you to new phases, God will oppose where you are, what you are doing, and how you are doing it. You will have to choose between God and your tradition.

I am in no way challenging you to change your message, your faith, your Christian beliefs or your doctrinal positioning. I am challenging you to change your posture toward God. Be willing to experience God in new, unexpected ways. God has always approached humanity in new ways. God is merely growing us up, requiring us to expand our understanding of God and welcome God's challenges to be transformed in to the likeness of Jesus Christ. We are not currently there. We have a way to go on this journey. You will find and follow God into truths that you have not grappled with. You will experience greater realities, new understandings, of God through the leading of the Holy Spirit in all of His fullness because you have embraced the challenge to change and grow in Christ.

Tradition vs Transformation

There is the issue of...
Tradition vs. transformation

In Genesis 12:1, Abraham was transformed by Faith. The Lord had said to Abram, "Go from your country, your people and your father's household to the land I will show you. (Genesis 12:1 NIV)

God had to get faith into Abraham. When God called Abraham to the Promised Land, he called him out of tradition. God called Abraham to get up and walk by faith to a land that God would show him. That was an act of faith. That was transformative.

Abraham was living with his family, in a cultural context where there was paganism all around. They sacrificed their children to unknown idol gods/ When God told Abraham to sacrifice his only son, then God showed up with a sacrifice, God was showing Abraham that God would provide. That was transformative. It was different from the tradition Abraham was used to. God is all about truth. God is greater than your tradition. Go after God. When you experience the greatest measure of His fullness, then discern if your tradition was a stepping stone, a tool, a resource, a blessing that helped you get closer to God. If not, ask yourself if it was a hindrance that prevented you from sensing, hearing, feeling, and knowing the God of your salvation and sanctification.

Go for God. Go after God!

All else are just slippery stones or stepping stones.

Moses – Transformed by Law

The LORD said to Moses, "Come up to me on the mountain and stay here, and I will give you the tablets of stone with the law and commandments I have written for their instruction." (Exodus 24:12)

There was lawlessness in the land

- God used the law to bring order and civility
- There is a place for government among men
- Government and civility is not the end for man. God requires more

Remember the creation story….

In the beginning God created the heavens and the earth. ² Now the earth was formless and empty, darkness was over the surface of the deep, and the Spirit of God was hovering over the waters. ³ And God said, "Let there be light," and there was light. ⁴ God saw that the light was good, and he separated the light from the darkness. ⁵ God called the light "day," and the darkness he called "night." And there was evening, and there was morning—the first day. ⁶ And God said, "Let there be a vault between the waters to separate water from water." ⁷ So God made the vault and separated the water under the vault from the water above it. And it was so. ⁸ God called the vault "sky." And there was evening, and there was morning—the second day. ⁹ And God said, "Let the water under the sky be gathered to one place, and let dry ground appear." And it was so. ¹⁰ God called the dry ground "land," and the gathered waters he called "seas." And God saw that it was good.

God created living things, then gathered these things together and separated them from other things and united some of them together. God creates His own law and then brings order.

Jesus – Transformed by Love

Leaving Nazareth, he went and lived in Capernaum, which was by the lake in the area of Zebulun and Naphtali. From that time on Jesus began to preach, "Repent, for the kingdom of heaven has come near." (Matthew 4:13, 17)

When Jesus stepped on the scene in Israel, the people, especially the religious leaders were all about their tradition. They had hardened hearts, and were sending empty prayers to a God who was not communicating back to them because their hearts were evil, and they were in a state of sin. Jesus stepped in and told them that they all needed to repent to God of their sin in order to prepare to hear from God. Now here Jesus is God about to speak to them, and He is telling them to get prepared because He will start speaking soon., but they were not apt, or open to transformation at that time, in that fashion. They could only see, hear or expect to experience God through their traditional way of doing things. Sometimes God uses tradition to get through to us. Sometimes God uses transformation. Sometimes tradition gets in the way of transformation. In seminary I learned that there are 3 components, or 3 things that are treated as truth. They are scripture, tradition, and experience. All are meant to help you wrestle with the movement and activity of God in your life.

Holy Spirit – Transformed by Power

But the fruit of the Spirit is love, joy, peace, forbearance, kindness, goodness, faithfulness, gentleness and self-control. Against such things there is no law. (Galatians 5:22-23)

When Jesus left and sent the Holy Spirit, God changed the game of life. He agreed to do all of the work. Our job is simply to surrender to it, allow the Holy Spirit to move through our heart. No longer are works good enough. Not only is faith enough. Now, it takes the welcoming of the invisible, the Holy Spirit of God who knocks on the door of our hearts with truth and grace. God transformed our world, and our lives one by one.

Transformers (14)

To become transformed, heed these points:

(1) Be committed to the God who transforms your life!

(2) Try God's way of doing things and be transformed

(3) Trust that there is always a more excellent way!

Salvation

God will do the work of saving you. He has figured out everything in your life. He has made plans, set aside blessings, and built bridges to connect the dots of your life. Now God is revealing Himself to you, little by little. If you would only believe God and begin to trust Him, He will show you where everything is, how to get to everything. He will show you what to do, and how to do it. God has everything planned out for you. He is only waiting for you to take the next step. It's like buying a model house that is all ready for you. All you have to do is put a down payment on it. And it's all yours. Just think! There is a life that is all yours.

Church Leadership

The difference between leadership in the church and leadership for the church is in your commitment. Leaders in the church bring their skills, abilities, and talents. They use them to lead others. Providing leadership, guidance and direction for the church is a little different though. It requires all of you. Providing leadership for the church requires a greater commitment. Is it in you? Are you ready? Great leaders are called to refocus their heart's commitment. When you refocus your energy, then the fruit of your labor and your long awaited blessing will follow.

Leaders

Leadership is not just owning a title, holding a position, or having the opportunity to tell others what to do. It is often the right, and responsibility to see what's wrong and then to fix it. If leadership responsibility has been bestowed upon you, or if you want to take the reins of leadership, then I challenge you. Take a long hard look at what is wrong, lacking, or ineffective right where you are. That will transform you into a leader, not by title, not by position, but by influence. Work with your current leaders to fix, or improve it what you've found.

The next level needs changers, the fixers, problem solvers, people with the vision to see what's wrong, the initiative to change the wrong, and the ability to see the wrong turn right, or at least better. The next level of leadership does not need hard workers alone. It needs hard workers and changers; do both and you will be an asset.

Love

Love is often based on feelings, on our sense of appreciation, and on the value we place on others. Someday our love grows up and becomes based on someone else's need until you love someone by meeting them at the point of their need. Here's God's love. You love someone by stepping out of the way, and allowing God to pour His love through your life and resources into someone else's life.

Do you really want to love others? What has God given you that will bless someone else? Ask God to identify your assets, the things you possess that others place value on. Then watch God bless others through you. That's love. Let your love grow and mature. Be committed to developing mature relationships with others.

Marriage

Love her! Love Him! You cannot change your spouse. You cannot force your spouse to become who you want them to be. You cannot change them into the perfect spouse. You cannot make them become any more like Christ than they are. It takes time. It takes the work of the Lord, and it takes patience. Transformative work is like surgery. Your job is to watch, pray, nurture, and encourage your spouse while the Lord transforms him or her into the likeness of Christ.

Husbands are required to wash their wives in the water of the word. Wives are required to submit to their husbands, love them and win them with meek humility. Then you will sanctify their souls. If you want to transform your spouse and transform your marriage, then patiently, wait, watch and pray. Jesus told His disciples to do the same as He was preparing to be arrested and taken away to be crucified. The disciples could not help him. They could not change Him. They could only watch, and pray.

Your spouse's next level and your marriage's next level are in your ability to love them unconditionally. Love them from the bad condition they are in today. Love them into the better condition they will be in tomorrow.

PARENTING

Don't spoil your kids with things. Don't make them rotten by merely giving them gifts, and taking them places to play. Children need parents to be more than enablers of fun. They need to do more than have a good time. Bless them intermittently with those things. Children are born with the natural ability and capacity to produce their own innocent joy all on their own. If you want to spoil them utterly rotten do so by engaging their spirit. Shower them with the Word. Let their minds grapple with the Word of God. Let their hearts sing the praises of God. Help them discern the will of God so they can also block attacks against the will of God in their lives.

If you want to spoil them, help them live in God's presence while they are still young. You will produce little David(s) who seek after God's own heart.

Friends

It is a blessing when you have a great family. Family is a mixture of differing personalities that are united under the common bond of blood relations. I've discovered something even greater than the gift of a close family. It is when you have a family of great friends. It is a blessing to go through life and discovering people of different backgrounds who have common values, interests, and desires as you. To call them friends is to build another family. It is a true gift of God.

Opportunities

Stay totally committed to where you are right now. Your next great opportunity usually comes after you totally buy in and sell out to where you are right now. Great opportunities usually find you after you've learned all you can and exhausted all of you have right where you are. They don't come just because you're tired of where you are.

Volunteering

Volunteering feels good. The charity of volunteer work benefits the giver and recipient of your labor. The challenge of volunteer work is that few people want to volunteer to do the work that needs a volunteer the most. I challenge you to find the hardest, most neglected, painful task that needs to be done. It's the thing that nobody else wants to do. Find it, volunteer to do it and make sure no one in has to worry about it because they know you have it under control. Others will honor you for it. They will probably remember you in the future when they need a dependable and honorable person. They may even recognize you for it publicly too.

Service

Do you have a knack for customer service? Do you like to help others find solutions? Keep improving on that. Strive to provide the best customer service in light site of where you are. Since everything revolves around people, know that you will get called, chosen, hired, promoted, and sought after by people with great needs and others with great authority if you put God first and His people 1st. You can always learn and develop the specialty skills needed to get the job done. It's the core values that get you in the conversation. Core competencies get you noticed. Core skills, like customer service make others realize you should be a part of the team.

Nearly every ministry, job, or opportunity involves people. Nearly every leader needs partners and teammates that know how you talk to people. They will look at your customer service to see if you are helpful to them and useful to the team (or partnership). Your customer service speaks to your ability to put other people first and yourself second. It is the determinant for ability to submit, surrender, be led, taught, and groomed for excellent service.

Skills

Whenever you start something new, know for sure that you will not begin it knowing all that you need to know. On your next assignment, remember you only need to know a little bit about it to get it, you only need to know a little more to start it. If you've already done a great job yesterday, then you have the potential to do a greater job tomorrow. Be confident that the God that was with you yesterday will supply all of your needs tomorrow. So don't worry if you don't have all of the skills you need today.

Give yourself time to develop them. Then when you have the time, learn all of the skills that you can, learn a little of everything. Master something. Then build a bond with1 greatly skilled leader and let them introduce you to opportunities where you will learn greater skills and greater opportunities where you will use them. Don't be afraid to step out in faith, just because you don't have <u>all</u> of the skills you need (already). Go ahead. Step out on faith. Shoot for the stars. Don't be scared.

Job hunting

If you are truly hungry, sometimes you have to apply everywhere. Apply for everything that looks interesting. Interview anyway even if you don't think you will get the job. Meet the hiring managers. Talk, listen, learn and get comfortable having conversations with the decision makers in your industry. They always know someone else or some place with a job opening for someone with your skills. They can help you find a niche. The person that doesn't have a job for you may help you find the one (1) 1 area that needs you the most. Start looking, applying, talking, listening and learning.

Needs

For basic survival, living creatures need air, water, and nutrients. When asked if they need anything, older people will often admit that all they really need is their family, friends and their health. For the Christian faith, all that was needed was the Father, Son and the Holy Ghost. The bible says we need faith, hope and love, and the greatest of these is love. Regardless of what you perceive your needs, you must remember to focus on them, with gratitude and forget the things that you don't have. Agonizing over the things you don't have will destroy you.

WHAT AM I DOING WITH MY TIME?

(Recovering my time with God)

The Problem is...

We don't know what we're supposed to be doing

The Solution is...

Jesus will call you to your purpose, & relationships

You will know what to do

The greatest commandments require love. God wants us to learn to love God. We will love God as a response to His love for us. Remember that loving God includes obeying God or it is not love at all. Loving God also requires loving others. Jesus asked how you can claim to love God whom you cannot see when you fail to love your brothers whom you do see.

It is assumed that you already love yourself. Now you must learn to love others as you love yourself. This love requires that you love others first. You must initiate this act of love, loving others completely. It requires that you empty yourself of your love, pouring it out on others.

That's the kind of love that God has showered you with. God loved you first. He initiated the act of love with you, then showered you with love, by sacrificing His Son for you. God wants your love to mature. You should love others even if it feels like it is killing you. We would call this loving unto death, or loving unto your own death in the flesh. For love gives life to others.

In a sense the lover experiences death in the flesh. Loving others is a cross, an act of crucifixion, a denial of self. That is a denial of your own selfish motives. When Jesus Christ died on the cross for us, it was an act of love, but He experienced death. It was the greatest act known to man. Jesus is calling you to love! You will have to long suffer, and endure people as you experience innumerable difficulties in your relationship with them. Yes, God is calling you to love God and others!

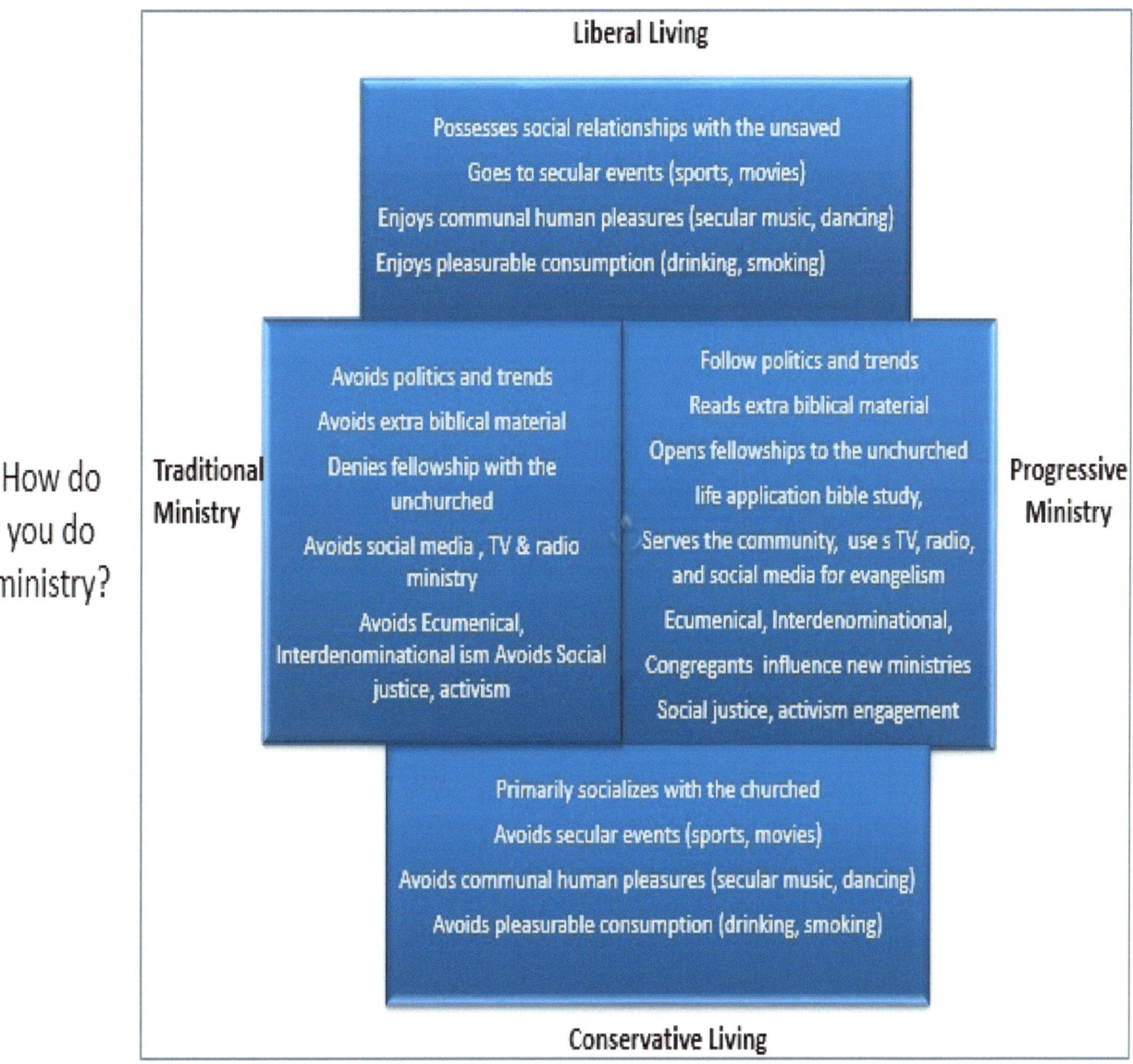

Live

- Liberal or Conservative?
- Social relationships with unsaved?
- Secular events (sports, movies)?
- Human pleasures (secular music, dancing)?
- Consumption (drinking, smoking)?
- Follow politics?
- Read extra biblical material?
- Opens fellowships to the unchurched?
- Support social media use?

Ministry

- Progressive or Traditional?
- Life application bible study?
- Social media use for evangelism?
- Street evangelism team?
- Have services in the community?
- Use of TV & radio, vs person to person invitations to discipleship?
- Ecumenical?
- Interdenominational?
- Congregants create or influence new ministries?
- Social justice, activism engagement?

When recovering, how will you spend your time?

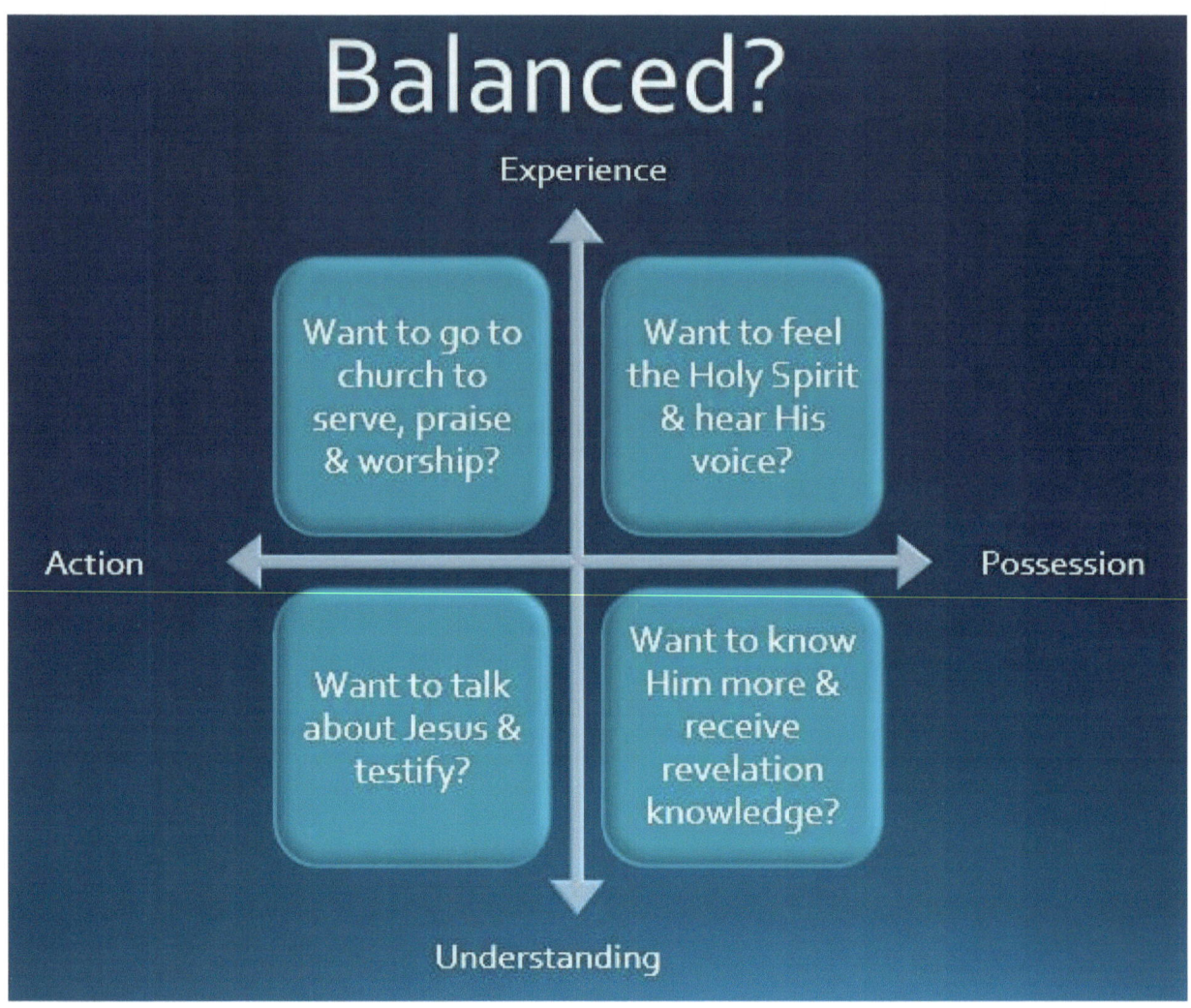

Why am I going through this?

(Understanding your suffering in Christ)

The Problem Is…

We don't know why we are here

The Solution Is…

God knows why we're here

The truth is that suffering is a part of our journey. This can be seen in the African American community's history with God as we've fought for emancipation, civil rights, and common dignity as a people. We've made it this far because God loves us, and cares for us. God has guided us, and sustained our efforts every step of the way. Today, our communities must realize that our present struggle against racially motivated violence is a part of a journey that was ordained for us to follow but the Lord will strengthen us to stand and walk by faith as we navigate these troubled waters.

Studying the life of Jesus teaches us that Jesus' journey led Him into some painful situations, persecution, and even crucifixion; therefore we should anticipate that our journey in Christ will lead us into some unpredictably painful situations as well. So that means that to follow Jesus, you must learn to suffer with Him.

Sometimes we suffer because we fail to follow Him, and sometimes we suffer because we do follow Him. God presents us with opportunities to proclaim our faith among the faithless, and to be a living witness of the living God for folks who need living proof that Jesus saves. But we forsake Jesus by dimming our light, shrinking away and choosing the path of easiest resistance. It later leaves us neck-deep in regret, reflecting on the path that we should have taken, wondering who we could have become, and how much stronger we would be if we stayed on the path and suffered just a little while with Jesus. Whatever situation you are in, sometimes you have to look at the challenge head on like Jesus and say, "not my will but thine be done" (Luke 22:42).

We have these questions when someone suffers:

1. HOW SHOULD I TREAT OTHERS?

2. HOW SHOULD OTHERS TREAT ME?

3. WHAT CAN OR SHOULD I EXPECT FROM OTHERS?

4. WHAT DOES GOD THINK ABOUT ME?

5. WHAT DOES GOD FEEL ABOUT ME?

6. WHAT DOES GOD SAY ABOUT ME?

7. WHAT DOES GOD KNOW ABOUT ME?

Here's what God wants you to do!

Know God

Love God

Love Others

Be a witness of God

Develop a disciplined life in Christ

Live by Grace

Have Mercy on others

Learn the scriptures; use them to inform your actions and behaviors

Be transformed

Develop Christian character

Fulfill the ministry of Jesus

Endure the suffering of Jesus

When am I going to find my way

The question is...

When will I find my way in Christ?

The answer is...

God is offering Spiritual Direction & Recovery

Let's read St John 5:16-18 (NIV)

So, because Jesus was doing these things on the Sabbath, the Jewish leaders began to persecute him. [17] In his defense Jesus said to them, "My Father is always at his work to this very day, and I too am working." [18] For this reason they tried all the more to kill him; not only was he breaking the Sabbath, but he was even calling God his own Father, making himself equal with God.

BACKGROUND

Israel had been 400 years without experiencing God's presence. They did not have the luxury, nor assurance that God was with them. Prior, God spoke to His people through His prophets. Now the prophets stopped speaking. Instead, God sent His one and only Son, who would do the speaking, heed the warning, and redirect the people to seek God with their hearts and return to Him. The religious leaders did not believe that Jesus was the Son of God, nor did they trust His words.

In John 5, we find Jesus performing miracles on the Sabbath. The Jewish leaders were upset for various reasons. First, they were upset that Jesus was performing miracles. For example, the crowds brought the blind, the lame, and the paralyzed to Jesus to be healed). Jesus healed the paralyzed man by telling him to pick up his mat and walk.

Second, he performed them on the Sabbath. Third, it was the Son of God that performed the miracles. Coming from God, He shared a commonality with God. This was insulting to them. These were the religious leaders! They should have known, believed in and followed God. For, these men did not believe in God. Their hearts were far from Him. It is very telling that the religious leaders were far from God. They could neither lead others to God, nor get to Him themselves.

As they began to persecute Jesus, out of their anger and resentment toward Him, Jesus answered them, saying, ""My Father is always at his work to this very day." That too is telling. Though God was silent for 400 years, God was still at work, preparing a life and a future for His people, both on earth and eternally. Though God stopped speaking through His prophets, He was preparing the stage for His Son. God was no longer sending them into exile, into the hands of their enemy nations as punishment for their sin and delivering them out of exile. Now God used John the Baptist to reveal their state of sin, and He sent Jesus as the way out. Only if God's leaders were willing to admit that they were in sin. Only if they were willing to admit that yes we are the leadership and we are no better off than the people we lead and serve.

It's funny, that if the leaders would have been praying for themselves, about their present state, then perhaps God would have revealed to them the state that they were in and that a way out was on the way. Unfortunately, the religious leaders were living pompous, presenting a lush religious lifestyle externally that was lifeless and dead on the inside. When the truth was revealed that they did not know God, they wanted to kill the truth. They could not kill God's truth. It was God in the flesh telling them the truth about themselves.

They could not stand (tolerate) the presence of God because they did not want to face the truth about themselves and their need for God's mercy. On the other hand, many of the more common Jews, who were not religious leaders, believed John the Baptist's message, repented, and were preparing themselves to receive the savior's love and to spend a life of faith in God. Meanwhile, the leaders remained in spiritual darkness, out in the cold, separated from the Love of God.

Let's look at them again….So, because Jesus was doing these things on the Sabbath, the Jewish leaders began to persecute him. [17] In his defense Jesus said to them, "My Father is always at his work to this very day, and I too am working." [18] For this reason they tried all the more to kill him; not only was he breaking the Sabbath, but he was even calling God his own Father, making himself equal with God.

Let's pull out Verse 16

"So, because Jesus was doing these things on the Sabbath"

Notice when this occurred.

- Remember the day (times)
- Remember the day you are living in (what day it is)
- They observed the Sabbath
- Jesus was doing things on the Sabbath
- Remember what the Day is for
- This is the day that the Lord has made
- This day this hour is for working
- Get to work today!

Let's look at Verse 17 - In his defense Jesus said to them, "My Father is always at his work to this very day, and I too am working."

This means that you will have to do a few things.

BE PREPARED FOR PERSECUTION

BE PREPARED FOR DEFENSE

- REMEMBER THE PLACE (SITUATION, E.G. SEPARATION)

- REMEMBER THE HOUR (MOMENT)

- REMEMBER WHO GOD IS

- REMEMBER THE TYPE OF GOD THAT YOU HAVE

    o FATHER @ WORK = JESUS WORKING

    o GOD IS YOUR FATHER (A LITTLE BIT OF GOD IN YOU)

Let's look at Verse 18

"For this reason they tried all the more to kill him; not only was he breaking the Sabbath, but he was even calling God his own Father, making himself equal with God."

LIVE

- It's life or death
- The world hates you
- The evil spirits at work in the world want to kill you
- With your sin and all, you must return to God
- Go get GOD!!!!

ABOUT THE AUTHOR

Dr. Derrick l Randolph, sr. Is from Baltimore, Maryland.

www.ingramcontent.com/pod-product-compliance
Lightning Source LLC
Chambersburg PA
CBHW041959150426
43194CB00002B/63

9 781944 166281